REAL ESTATE BUILDING THE BASICS

Jennifer G

Copyright © 2014 Jennifer G

All rights reserved.

Illustrated by © Chuyu
Dreamstime.com - Urban Forest New Real Estate Buildings Photo

ISBN: 1502953811

ISBN-13: 978-1502953810

*Home is where your heart is.   Land is where you build.
Together your heart will be built to satisfaction.*

Table of Contents

PART ONE - Relationship Utilized	6
Chapter 1 - Identity	8
Chapter 2 - Tools of the Trade	12
Chapter 3 - A Little Extra	16
PART TWO - Productivity	18
Chapter 4 - What's Expected	20
Chapter 5 - Marketing	24
PART THREE - Self Profit	28
Chapter 6 - Price Fixing	30
Chapter 7 - Misrepresentation	34
Chapter 8 - Group Boycott	38
Chapter 9 - Kickbacks	42
Chapter 10 - Redlining	46
Chapter 11 - Steering	50
Chapter 12 - Blockbusting	56
PART FOUR - The Contract	60
Chapter 13 - Before	62
Chapter 14 - During	66
Chapter 15 - Final	72
PART FIVE - Home Responsibilities	74
Chapter 16 - Property Value	76
Chapter 17 - Maintenance & Upgrade	82
Chapter 18 - Using Your Home	86
Chapter 19 - Your Next Move	90
PART SIX - The Story	92
Chapter 20 - In Debra's Favor	94

PART ONE

Relationship Utilized

Chapter 1

Identity

Independent Contractor

An independent contractor means that you are in business for yourself. This may be confusing in the real estate industry if you are an agent. Agents sometimes are *treated* as if they are employees when they are not. An employee gets a paycheck from their employer. Agents get a 1099 at the end of the year, if they have made a sale. There are no benefits, no overtime, and no scheduled hours for independent contractors. They work exclusively on their own under the Brokers guidance.
Things get muddied when Brokers take matters in their own hands and start making demands on agents to comply with their stringent rules. Brokers may require an agent to attend office meetings, perform open houses, take turns managing the front desk, wear a company jacket, run personal errands for them, and manage agency's marketing materials. An agent, who feels that they are being treated as an employee, should discuss this matter with the broker for resolution. An agent should spend the time to grow their own business and not the business of the agency. The agency's business will grow in accordance with the performance and production of the agents.
If the problem of identity cannot be resolved, it may be time to find another broker to work with.

Agent

What is a real estate agent? It is a person who represents their clients in a transaction for a commission. They also must work with an agency and must be licensed. They are classified as an independent contractor. They must abide by the law and practice by ethical means. Their purpose is to provide the best possible service to their clients.

Agents do not have a set working schedule. Because they get a 1099, they are in essence in business for themselves. They set their own hours. They have their own expenses; their broker is not responsible for supplying them with any marketing materials. They must not co-mingle their personal funds with business funds. They should be respectful to the clients' needs and requests. Although it is not required, they should dress professionally. In some cases, agency's requires that they do. They should be familiar with the current real estate law and any newsworthy events pertaining to the industry. In other words, don't be out of the loop.

Broker

A broker in the real estate industry has the right to represent the buyer or the seller in a real estate transaction. They manage agents within the agency. They are licensed differently than an agent and normally has higher income stream, more business responsibilities, and they can do business on their own as an agency establishment; compared to an agent who cannot work independently without a broker.

They have the ability to collect a negotiated commission percentage, from an agent's transaction. Brokers are not automatically owners of an agency. A real estate agency can have an owner that knows nothing about real estate, but the owner must have a broker in order to conduct business. A broker is a key essential person in running a real estate business. They are the go to person for mostly everything in that business. The Board of Realtors is another avenue for providing assistance, but normally they will redirect you back to the broker.

Dual Agency

Dual agency is when you represent both the buyer and the seller in the same transaction. This is a tricky position to be in and is highly not recommended. You must represent both sides without sharing confidential information or violating the respective parties. It is wise to practice due diligence at all times. If you feel that entering into a dual agency relationship is compromising your position, you should request that another agent represent one of your clients and share the commission.

This relationship also occurs when two agents from the same agency represents a buyer and a seller respectively for the office listing. For example, a walk in buyer may be interested in an office listing where they may hire another office agent to represent them.

Dual agency must be disclosed to both parties in writing, where all participants must sign the relationship agreement. No matter if you are a broker or an agent, you must be careful with the liabilities pertaining to dual agency.

Chapter 2

Tools of the Trade

Exclusive Right to Sell &

Exclusive Right to Represent

As an agent you should always ask your client if they had signed an exclusive right to sell agreement with another agent. This listing agreement assures that the agent will get their commission regardless if the seller seeks assistance from another agent. You do not want to work hard for a client and not get paid. If your client has this agreement with another agent, that agent will get paid regardless if you made the transaction happen AND most importantly you may not get paid for your effort. In most cases, sellers can't turn around and try to sell their own property without paying you while this agreement is in effect. Always do due diligence and check this important fact. If the agreement expired, then you should engage in one for yourself to ensure compensation. This agreement is nearly iron clad.

An exclusive right to represent basically works in the same manner as the right to sell, except for the fact that you are representing buyers.

Multiple Listing Service

MLS (multiple listing service) is a service provided through your Board of Realtors to have a centralized regional listing base. It provides an avenue for all agents and brokers to list properties from their agency and share it with one another. This sharing allows more visibility and promotes transactions to occur. Most people, now, are searching the Internet for homes and in some cases are listing their homes without an agent. Some agents still find the MLS useful. There are more detailed information and notes that may not be obtainable over the Internet. Also, commission rates are disclosed on the MLS. The MLS may have access to acquiring property tax information. Furthermore, not all clients want their property information made available over the Internet. For example, some sellers don't want a for sale sign on their property or their neighborhood may forbid it. In addition, there may be a high profile client who does not wish to reveal that they are selling their property to the general public. In such cases, an MLS is very useful.

Disclosure Form

This form explains the defects of the property or any relating pertinent matter involving the property. Such matters may include appliance defects, relevant improvements to property (new roof), any structural damages, underground tanks, moisture or mold problems, foundation issues, and any problems that may not be visible or found during inspection. For example, sellers should disclose if there is a nearby nuclear power plant. Issues on a disclosure form may be the deciding factor of whether a buyer proceeds with purchasing the property.

If a major hurricane or earthquake occurred which resulted in minor damages to the property, it must be disclosed. Although it may be minor, future problems may occur to the buyer. If a buyer is still interested in the property both the seller and the buyer should sign to acknowledge that the form was completed. Usually the seller has one already prepared and signed.

Sales Contract

The real estate sales contract outlines the details of the purchase. It should have the property address, purchase price, any deposit, appraisal, inspections, any fixtures that may be omitted from the sale, and when the buyer can take possession of property, closing costs, and other legal information, and both buyer and seller signatures. Verbal contracts should not be accepted, but unfortunately some parts of the sales contract are verbally communicated. For example, a buyer may want to keep a chandelier as part of the property which the seller agrees upon. This agreement may not be outline in the written sales contract. When this occurs, and the seller does not comply it becomes disputable. It is always smart to have everything in writing.

It becomes more important when a seller agrees in writing to make improvements prior to the sale and the buyer finds out that it was not done or it wasn't done correctly. The buyer can hold the seller responsible by using the sales contract. The seller must then re-mediate the buyer at their own expense. This saves the buyer from burdensome expenses. To reiterate, putting every detail in writing is vital.

Chapter 3

A Little Extra

Reciprocity

Reciprocity is when you have obtained a licensed in one state and can use it in other participating states; by getting a reciprocal license. This way you do not have to take multiple examinations and multiple continuing education requirements. Of course, your license must be good standing and you must be working with an agency.

Usually, agents with reciprocity do business in neighboring states. It helps when they have clients who are looking to relocate. Each state has its special qualifications that you must adhere to. You must verify which states that share reciprocity with your licensed state. For example, New York may have reciprocity with Pennsylvania, but does not with Florida. It's good to know this, because you clearly must handle a client transaction different if the client wishes to retire in Florida from New York. In such a case, a referral may be the best way to handle it.

Errors and Omissions insurance

Errors and omissions insurance, also known as professional liability insurance, covers the cost of any mistakes that a real estate agent may embark upon. It does not mean that you are not liable. It does not mean you can act in a careless manner. You must still try to perform your business with due diligence. This insurance is added security for the broker when an agent makes a legal mistake. New agents may be more prone to making mistakes involving the laws and ethics. Sometimes, agents do not act professionally when they are working with family, friends, and close colleagues. When doing business with people you know personally, you should put forth a professional conduct.

Note, that an agent may still be legally liable for any wrong doing in lieu of any insurance. Lawsuits by clients and other agents still can be pursued. Agents do sue other agents when there is a disputable transaction involving commissions and representations. Furthermore, no one is exempt from legal ramifications, when the rights of the protected class have been violated.

PART TWO

Productivity

Chapter 4

What's Expected

Appearance

      Presentation is important when you are an agent. You want your clients to see you as a professional person. You want them to feel confident that they are working with someone who is responsible and knows what they are doing. If you have a questionable appearance they may not want to work with you. Keep in mind every location has its own culture. There are some areas where agents present themselves very casually, while other areas they present themselves very formally.

      Working in the city is very much different than working in the country. If you are in an area where you are getting your feet and attire dirty, you may want to dress casually when showing homes. If you are in a market area where style and appearance are always being judged, you may want to dress formally or have a uniform. Outside of what you are wearing, your appearance should be neat. No matter what your style you should not be dis-shuffled or look remotely disorganized. You can wear the most expensive formal attire and still look disarranged. No client wants to see their agent as not prepared, not ready, and confused. Looking the part and acting the part emphasizes confidence. When an agent appears to be confident, the clients will also be confident that they will find their dream home.

      In summary, an agent's appearance is a representation of

their business. Each agent is their own business.

Sales Goals

One important goal is your sales goals. How much money do you want to make? What are your goals in the real estate industry? Is it a temporary or permanent move? Having the answers to these questions will improve your vision of what you must do to achieve them. A good exercise would be to write your answers down and work it out step by step. As tedious as this may be, it can help you make your goals come to reality. It is seeing each step play out and making sure that all steps are covered.

We can look at the monetary projection you want to make in sales and we can look at how much number of sales you would like to make. Simply by making a formula for the year.

What is the number of sales you would like to achieve?
1) House sales = 12
2) Condo sales = 12
3) Co-op sales = 6
4) Rentals = 30

Then figure out what you have to do in order to achieve these goals. What steps are needed to sell a property?
1) Prospecting
2) Marketing materials
3) Follow up communication
4) Required documents, presentation and signing
5) Open houses
6) Listing property

Now you have to figure out the amount of hours you are going to need to spend in order to achieve your goals. Working part time with about 20 hours a week may not produce the outcome you want. Whether you have another job, you may need to put in full time hours in order to accomplish your goals at hand. Another option is to adjust your goals to something that is more realistic.

Since you have looked into what you want to accomplish, and wrote it down. Then you can add value to it.

How much money would you like to achieve for the amount of sales you expect to engage in?
1) House sales = 12 = $6,000,000 sales amount
   (average house sale = $500,000)
2) Condo sales = 12 = $3,600,000 sales amount

(average condo sale = $300,000)
3) Co-op sales = 6 = $1,200,000 sales amount
(average co-op sale = $200,000)
4) Rentals = 30 = $54,000 rental amounts
(average rental = $1,800)

Now you have a projected sales amount prior to your commission. If you are splitting commission with listing agent and your broker, you net commission may be considerably lower than expected. If you look at the net commission for each projected sales goals, your new projection would be as follows. Take in consideration that these are estimates depending upon commission rates and other variables.

1) House sales = $90,000 commission
2) Condo sales = $54,000 commission
3) Co-op sales = $18,000 commission
4) Rentals = $13,500 commission

You expected goal may total to $175,500 for the year. To some this may not be realistic. To others it is attainable. It all depends on how much effort your put into it, your clientele, and your location. Some agents make a fraction of this commission, while others may make multiple times more than the commission. Do what's best for you and readjust your goals as needed. A yearly reevaluation of your goals helps keep things in perspective.

Communication Skills

People come from various backgrounds and cultures. They communicate with one another to express their needs, desires, and wants. Sometimes people misinterpret what is said and what is done. It is not advisable to bring slang and unwanted body language into your profession. What may come natural to you and that is not offensive to you, may be very offensive to clients and others that you may work with. Keep in mind that this world is shared by many different backgrounds that have different interpretations. To resolve any communication issues, one should try to express themselves in a different manner. Simply put, communication can be a problem if not understood.

Agents should keep the line of communication always open. Technology can be used to alleviate any communication issues. Clients can use the Internet, cell phones, faxes, and phones to communicate with their agents. There should be no reason why a client can't get in touch with you. As a matter of fact, that is not usually the problem. Getting in touch is not as much a problem as the timeliness of the response. Clients may complain that their agent does not respond in a timely manner, especially, when time is of an essence when making an offer. Agents must move fast in responding to clients, agents, and brokers when working on a transaction. If an agent moves too slowly, they may miss the opportunity of obtaining their clients dream home. Even if the agent cannot reach their client immediately, they should make every attempt to use due diligence in performing the task at hand. Putting in an offer, scheduling a viewing, counter-offering, and documents must be processed in a timely manner and accurately. Accurately is the key word that involves clear communication with all parties.

To sum up, look before you leap in terms of communication. Look at how you are speaking and presenting yourself. Ask yourself if it is acceptable by the industry. Ask yourself if it is correct and non-offensive. Then move forward.

Chapter 5

Marketing

Sphere of Influence

You probably heard the phrase sphere of influence before. Who you know and personal connections play a key role, as well, in your marketing. You need a marketing agenda to get started. But before that the easiest and the most available are the people close to you. Your day to day friends and family, your religious affiliations, your club members, etc. Because you know them already, it is easiest to communicate with them; and they are much more attainable. In a friendly conversation or a friendly email let them know that you are an agent now and you can help them with their needs.

A lot of agents start out part time, because they do not want to leave their full time job for a commissioned pay. Therefore, this career may be another source for extra income. Whatever the reasons, your co-workers at your 9-5 can also know that you are an agent. Bring it up in conversation. Having a business should not be a secret.

Marketing Materials

As an agent, your broker that you work for is going to demand you make good deals. No one wants a dead beat agent taking up space. There are many people entering this business as agents every day. Not everyone that enters make it in the industry. Therefore there is a turnover rate that needs to be considered as a business owner. Your goal is to remain in the industry and remain successful.

Since you're getting a 1099 at the end of the tax year, you are not considered an employee. This means that a lot of the cost involved in becoming productive comes from you. There are some agencies that help their agent get started. They may help you with your mailings and getting your business cards, but most are not going to hold your hands along the entire way. This is a competitive marketplace and it wouldn't be fair to help one agent out and not all. Because the startup cost can be cumbersome when you are not readily receiving any income, most agents prefer that their broker help them defray some costs.

Years ago business cards were pretty standard. They came with the basics, your name, business name, address, logo, phone and fax. Now the cards have options where you can add your mobile phone, round the corners, have various background pictures and slogans and alternatives like appointments on the back of the card. In some cases business cards can be electronic for the Internet savvy people. Your business card is a marketing tool. You should give it out to everyone you can, whether you are in a general conversation with someone or are actually speaking about real estate. You should somehow state that you are a real estate agent and you are available to help anyone in need of your business. If it is declined, you should insist that they pass on your business card to friends they may know. Word of mouth is still a strong marketing avenue. Don't give up, be persistent.

Working with Vendors

Lots of time there are vendors looking to sell their products to agents. They gain and you gain if their product works well for you. There are software programs that can manage your clients, your costs and you commission, and also helps you schedule appointments and take notes regarding your work. If you use it to its full capacity you may find that it makes doing your work a lot easier where you can focus on getting more clients. Either you can be organized and make your life easier or you can be disorganize and rough things through. How you do your work will affect how productive you become. Being an agent means that you are a professional. Being a professional requires responsibilities of which being organized is one of them.

Your Website & The Internet

Most agents have websites of their own. A broker may have restrictions on how agents display their website. So it is highly recommended that they get approval from their broker to make sure they don't have anything that may become a legal issue. Some agents have made mistakes by putting up someone else's listing on their site, feeling that it is OK, since it came from the same office.

It is never OK to take someone else's listing for any reason. As an agent, unless your name is on the listing, you cannot use that listing as if it is yours. Listings are hard to come by. There is a bunch of work in getting a listing; therefore, no one should have that stolen from them. Websites can also help in getting a listing because some have the ability to have viewers add their contact information and they can get notices from you. For example, you can send them newsletters.

Someone can look at your website and see one of your just sold listings. They may be able to leave their contact information to have you send more information to their email. They can also have notifications on the home search criteria that they were looking for. Some people's criteria is very specific and require a lengthier search, which takes much more time and effort than someone who is just looking for a flat they can afford. Most websites draws in lots more buyers than sellers. There are plenty of people now-a-days that go on-line to look for homes while sellers may opt to go to their local real estate agency to list their property. Make note that the Internet has educated buyers and sellers and knows a lot about the real estate industry. You don't want to get in a situation when your clients know more than you do, so educate yourself to know more than them. Your edge is that you know more about the legal aspects of the industry. They may know the different types of homes, the area, and the "look" of the home. They may know what's on the surface but not what's underneath, so to speak. A savvy buyer may investigate on-line the different things they may run into when buying a home. They may want to know about asbestos, the year the home was built, etc. It is your job to provide them with what information is required so that they may make a smart decision. Holding information back to make a sale is discouraged and may be illegal. Ethical behavior is strongly recommended. No one wants to be misrepresented.

One thing that some agents don't do is update their website. Your website is a representation of your business. If you do not periodically update the website, it may become non-competitive. A website must attract people and it must have them keep coming back to it. Changing it up with things that may be useful for clients is highly recommended. Adding financial tools, helpful links, and making it user friendly are always a plus. You don't want too much clutter on your website, where it becomes hard to even look at. Your website is like your store. Your main page is like your store front. You should make it inviting.

PART THREE
Self Profit

Chapter 6

Price Fixing

The Scenario

Have you ever gone shopping for utility service and everywhere you go is the same price or relatively the same? Ever wonder if these companies know each other's price? Well, if they do know each other and agreed to set the price, it is price fixing. Price fixing is illegal. It prevents fair competition and in some cases creates monopolies. If you're caught you are definitely doing jail time. In the real estate business, you could be preventing clients from getting fair market value.

Timothy normally goes to the annual real estate expo to learn about anything new in the real estate industry. He, also, loves networking with other agents. He's interested in relocating his business to another state, so it's important for him to network and find out how others are doing in their location. He met Tony at the expo and they began to talk about their business in their respective location. It turns out that Tony works for a local realty near Timothy. He's new to the industry and inexperienced.

"How do you make it in this business successfully? It's harder than I thought." Tony said.

"It's not a big deal. Before you know it, it would be second nature. Just hang in there." Timothy reassured him. Timothy wanted to grow his market. He was tired of dealing with other agents and their chants about "this is my territory". He didn't want to deal with that nonsense. It's stupid how some agents take their territory so seriously and so revengeful. One agent had the audacity to put a nasty note on his car to stay out of her territory and stop marketing in her area or else.

"Yeah, but you have to have a secret to success. Tell me man, what's yours?" Tony insisted.

"I have no secret. I just work real hard. It's just a competitive industry. That's all." Timothy replied.

"Well, what do you charge? What's your commission base? Do you negotiate differently with higher end clienteles? My broker allows us to do whatever." Tony said.

"I don't know anything about your broker. But as you do well in the business, you have more flexibility in negotiating your commission. Why do you ask?" Timothy said coyly. He had an idea. Since, Tony was in the same local market territory, he may strike a deal with him. Tony wouldn't know any better. Timothy would be able to expand his market territory before Tony figures out what is going on. Then he will change his strategy before getting caught. It would be simple and successful.

"So you do negotiate higher commission with clients who have money?" Tony asked.

"Look... if you need help the person you should be asking is your broker. I shouldn't be talking to you about commissions. But to tell you the truth, I am planning to become a broker next year. I've fulfilled the requirements already. If you're not satisfied where you are at, then you may want to switch agencies." Timothy said.

"Really? I heard about your agency. They are doing pretty well. But why would they want me. They seem very competitive with picking top agents. I'm new." Tony said.

"We were all once new. I started just like you and was trained right. The problem is if you start at an agency that doesn't teach you the tricks of the trade; you would just end up as just a number. A number lost in the real estate industry doesn't make much money. You know what I mean?" Timothy said.

"Yeah... I think so." Tony said. He thought that he should move to a better agency if he wanted to make it.

"Here's my business card. If you're thinking about moving now, I can speak to my broker about signing you." Timothy said. "As for the commission, I set my commission depending upon the selling price."

"Really?" Tony waited for him to tell him more, but

expected nothing. After a moment of silence, he realized that Timothy was waiting on him to respond to his offer. "I am thinking about moving." Tony said.

"Good. But can you make the grade? Do you think you have what it takes to work with our agency?" Timothy asked.

"Yes, of course. I'm a quick learner." Tony said.

"OK, prove it. In the next three months, let's see how much you can make. To start let's see if you can negotiate a commission fee of 7.5%. If you can successfully do this, then I will guarantee a place in our agency. That's my promise." Timothy said.

Tony thought about it. If he can pull it off, it would be a win win in his case. He would earn a larger commission than his low 6% and he would move in to one of the best agencies in the area. He can't lose.

"OK. I'll do it." Tony said while looking at Timothy's well spent business card.

Timothy had him. For the next three months they both had the same commission rate and were able to lock in their target territory. Timothy later became broker of his own business and decided to expand with Tony. Tony agreed that they would work together as independent agents in two different territories where they were engaged in setting the price. They plan to both grow their business and after having a successful growth, they would eventually merge to one agency and lock the market.

The Test

Timothy and Tony had successful grown their agencies and is now ready to merge and lock the market. Unfortunately, rumor has it they were engaging in price fixing on various levels. Testers decided to investigate to put a stop to it. Tony and Timothy were into living well with high end clienteles. They weren't thinking about testers or getting caught. As a matter of fact they knew other agents that did the same things that they did. They had no worry in the world.

An investigation was done and they were found guilty of price fixing. They both denied price fixing. What do you think they should do?

1. Shred all their documents regarding their sales for the past seven years.

2. Make a deal with the prosecutors and rat out the others who engaged in price fixing.
3. Plead guilty and suffer the consequences.
4. Put all their assets in the loved ones name, and move their money to a secure off shore account.
5. Kill themselves, because they can't take the pressure and they rather die than go to jail.

Chapter 7

Misrepresentation

The Scenario

Have you ever went on vacation and realized that what you expect and what you experienced was vastly different? The advertisement said the hotel had a pool, walking distance to beach, close to shopping, air conditioning and free Wi-Fi. When you get there it does not have a pool, it's a driving distance to the beach, no shopping nearby, a ceiling fan, and no Wi-Fi. In this case, its false advertisement, but the concept of being deceived is there. What you expect and what you got were two different things. The hotel should not have misrepresented itself for having the attributes it said it had, when indeed it didn't have any of it.

Gladys and Monica were doing an open house. Gladys is a licensed real estate agent and Monica was an assistant with no license. Monica was helping Gladys with the open house. She helped set up the refreshments, put up the yard signs, and provided the contact sheets. Gladys wanted Monica to meet and greet clients at the door and have them wait if she was already engaged in showing the property. The house was fairly marketed and there was a good turnout. Monica had difficulty keeping the prospects waiting and Gladys gave her the go ahead to show the house as well.

"I can show you upstairs, once my colleague finishes." Monica said. The couple she was speaking to was getting restless. There were two other couples waiting to see the house and they were all eager to make an offer.

"OK. Do you know if there is room for negotiation?" The buyer asked.

"Well, It's not my listing. But you should put in an offer if you're interested. I suggest a good offer." Monica said.

"OK." The buyers said.

"There have already been three other offers presented." Monica said. She noticed that Gladys was coming downstairs with buyers. "I can show you the upstairs now."

"OK." The buyers said. Monica showed the rest of the house to them. She was well educated in the real estate business and knew about all the forms. She presented the forms to the buyers and asked them if they wanted to put in an offer before they leave.

"I have the paperwork, if you want to put in an offer. All offers will be presented to the sellers today. They are eager to sell, so I highly recommend that you move on this as soon as possible." Monica explained. The buyers agree to put in an offer.

"Do you have a business card?" the buyers asked.

Monica pretended to look for her business card. "I'm sorry. I'm all out, but you can call the office and ask for me or Gladys. We are working together." Monica said. She shook their hands and proceeded to walk them out.

The next day, Monica's buyers offer got accepted. Gladys realized that the terms on the offer were incorrect and told Monica. She said that Monica should call the buyers and tell them that they would have to agree to the correct terms if they wanted to make the purchase. Monica called and told the buyers that their offer is accepted but the terms were incorrect. She said in order to go through with the purchase they would have to agree to the correct commission fee. The buyers complained that it was not fair and it was not their fault. They refused and said they will still like to continue with the purchase since it's been accepted. Gladys told Monica that the seller would have to go with the next best offer, because she will not agree with the incorrect commission fee. Gladys then told the seller that the initial accepted offer had been rescinded and that they should consider the next best offer. The seller agreed.

The Test

Monica's buyers found out that the property was sold to someone else. They decided to pursue a lawsuit against the agency. They later found out that Monica is not a licensed agent. What should the agency do?
1. Tell the buyers that Monica is not a real agent and therefore no real offer took place.
2. Settle the legal case with the buyers.
3. Fire Gladys and Monica for misrepresentation and tainting the agency's reputation.
4. Fire Monica and keep Gladys, because Gladys didn't force Monica to go that extra step.

Chapter 8

Group Boycott

The Scenario

No one likes gangs, especially when they are bullied by them. They value their own ideology and are extremely selfish people. They acquire more people in their gang when they pressure others to join in; they just are afraid to deal with the leader. No one wants to be bullied, not even their members. As adults in the professional industry, it is your responsibility to make an initiative to follow the laws. You should respect the space and the rules of others. You should be responsible and give others a chance to engage in fair competition.

Melissa had buyers who were interested in a listing of Homes Realty. She worked for Adrienne's Realty. Homes Realty had an unspoken policy of a set commission rate that Adrienne's Realty did not participate in. Melissa scheduled to show the listing to her buyer.

"So the appointment is set for Saturday at 11am." Melissa confirmed.

"Yes, there will be no problem. I will let the tenants know that they should make the place available for that time." Jim said. Homes Realty policy is to notify any tenants at least one day notice for showing. They did not have any problem showing that property because the renters were very nice.

Saturday at 11am, Melissa tried to show the property. There was no lock box. She was instructed to confirm appointment, in which she did, and to just show up. Melissa rang the bell and knocked on the door as her client waited with her to get in. No one came to open the door. She saw that someone was home, because the children were playing outside in the front and the back. She asked the children to get their parents so that she can speak to them. They did, but Melissa was told that they did not know of any showings for that day and they could not let them in.

Melissa called Homes Realty to explain what happened. They apologized and said they can reschedule the showing.

Next week, Melissa tried again to show the property and this time no one was home. She called Homes Realty again and no one picked up. She left a message reminding them of her appointment that she confirmed. The same clients were with her and were getting frustrated. They thought she was incompetent and no longer wanted to work with her or her agency.

Melissa went back to the office and complained about her treatment from Homes Realty. Jim said that he has always had a problem showing Homes Realty listings. They realized that Homes Realty was just not interested in doing business with Adrienne's Realty. In fact, they realized that Homes Realty and Top Hill Realty had locked that territory and made it difficult for other agency's that did not comply with their commission split and terms.

The Test

Jim and Melissa decided that Homes Realty and Top Hills Realty were unfair. Melissa had lost her clients and was very angry over the incident. Jim had also lost clients because of Top Hills Realty. Their broker, Susan, preferred to do nothing and told them to focus on their own affairs. Susan had already tried, with no solution, to report Homes and Top Hills realty. Unfortunately, they had connections with the Board of Realtors. In fact, she started having difficulty doing business, because of their connections.

Melissa knew other agents that were fed up with their actions and wanted to put a stop to it. These agents were more than willing to engage. They were willing to form a boycott against them out of retaliation.

What do you think they should do?

    1. Collude with other agents from other agencies to

prevent agents from Homes and Top Hills Realty from showing any of their listings.
2. Collude with other agents to not accept any offers from Homes and Top Hills Realty, out of retaliation.
3. Report Homes and Top Hills Realty, to prevent them from continuing with their tactics.
4. Start soliciting as many of Homes and Top Hills realty clients to steal their market and take over their territory.

Chapter 9

Kickbacks

The Scenario

As a real estate agent, you earn your money when you make a sale. Your office may consider rewarding top sellers or top listers with a favorable percentage breakdown. Instead of the sad 50/50 breakdown between the agent and the broker, they may opt to give 70/30. The more you sell the more they want to encourage you to continue selling; and they want to secure that you stay at their agency. Understandably, top agents are highly sought after. Sometimes bonuses are implemented in the commission process to encourage and accelerate transactions. But sometimes agents take it too far. Sometimes agents won't do what they are supposed to do unless they are getting a little extra in return. Sometimes agents won't go that extra mile without a little something in their pocket. They consider this as going to make them the winner, that is, the biggest bread winner. When they go too far and get caught doing so, they risk losing their licenses and they may even tarnish the agency's reputation.

There are some agents that are clever enough to get kickbacks without getting caught. Making a winning sale and then getting referrals from your clients is a natural process. Some agents take it too far and give money for these referrals, which is how they generate more business. It's how they become the biggest bread winner. Sending clients to a mortgage broker so that the agent can then receive a percentage of the commission on approved mortgages, is how some engage in kickbacks. Kickbacks can come in various forms and gifts. Kickbacks can even be favors, such as picking up the marketing expenses that would have otherwise been incurred by an agent.

Steven, an agent at Little Town Realty, obtained a new client that was heavily involved in her church. Crystal, was in the choir, taught Sunday school, and was involved in every church activity she could get into. She knew practically everyone at her church. She often said "praise the lord" and "thank you Jesus" when in conversation. Steven was very happy to have her as a client. To him, her church had affluent members.

"I'm so glad you found me this place. I was looking for a new home for a while now. I don't want to be too far from my church and it's been very hard." Crystal said.

"I know it can be difficult. There isn't much activity in that part of town, but knowing the right people helps." Steven said.

"Thank you Jesus." Crystal said.

"Please pass my business card along. You see on the back of it says 'referrals are kindly accepted'". Steven said.

"Oh. Yes. I know a lot of people. My lovely church sister is looking for a better place. I'll give her this card." Crystal said.

"Please do. I'll tell you between me and you." He whispered. "I can donate money to your church for every person you refer me, that becomes a successful client." Steven said.

"Oh, praise the lord." Crystal said. She nodded in agreement.

Steven received a lot of clients from Crystal's church. His business grew considerably after that. He kept up with donations to churches, nonprofit organizations, breast cancer awareness, and other gifts in exchange for successful referrals.

The Test

You have a working relationship with a mortgage lender, Bill. He feels that he can trust you and bring you into the loop. Bill has been building his business successfully for many years, slowing bringing agents into his scheme. During a lunch meeting, he makes an offer to you. For every successful client you send him, he'll give you part of his fee in cash. He didn't want anything on the books and no necessary future conversation on this subject. It would just be understood from this point on. In addition he will host seminars on the mortgage process for prospective buyers for an extremely discounted cost. Bill offered to share the client list from the seminars. He stated he will cover the marketing materials and advertising costs for these seminars. His offers sound very lucrative to you. It appears that Bill will be doing most of the work and all you have to do is provide the clients and share them. In fact, the broker does not have to know anything about the details of the deal. It would be an exclusive relationship where you didn't have to share any of the money with the broker, like you do with the commissions. You're thinking that building your clientele and gaining more exclusive money would grow your business faster so that one day you can become a broker.

What do you do?

1. Say forget it. You're nervous that he may steal your clients and share it with other agents that he also has good relationships with.
2. Say yes. No one can track cash gifts. No one will notice something is going on. And your growth will be quicker.
3. Tell your broker about his offer, because you don't want to get in any trouble. You're nervous that someone may be setting you up for trouble.
4. Negotiate the conditions and ask for more money. You know that Bill just isn't right and he may be doing business with other agents. You know that you want to be the top agent, so your deal should be better than the rest.

Chapter 10

Redlining

The Scenario

Now a days there are a variety of different kinds of loans to meet your needs. There is something for everyone. But what if you just can't get a loan? What if your options are limited? Have you ever tried to get a loan, where you thought you met all the criteria only to find you hit a road block? Have you ever got frustrated and wondered if it is really your fault or just the system? Well, think again. Do a thorough analysis, because it may not be your fault at all.

Years ago, when discrimination was at the highest, in your face, and culturally declared, banks used to literally outline areas designating where people can live based on race and ethnicity. It was a cruel and unjust behavior, but it existed. The government put a stop to this, but it doesn't mean that some people will still try to use this concept to continue discrimination.

A young, newly married and recent MBA graduates decided to buy a house together. They both make about $250,000 a year and have decided to start their own business in rental properties. Laverne has good credit and her husband Barney has fair credit. Barney, while in college, had messed up his credit and is now trying to build his credit. Their plan is to buy a fixer upper in a promising neighborhood. They will fix the rental property and rent it out for a good investment return. They have an appointment with Harry's Mortgage Services.

"Good day and welcome. Please sit down." Harry sat them down in his meeting room where they went over what they qualified for. Laverne wasn't too happy with the results.

"Is that it? I know we said we were thinking of getting a fixer upper, but we still wanted to start our investment with room to renovate in a high end market. I don't think the number we qualified for gives us that opportunity to do so." Laverne was very concerned with the low mortgage number that Harry gave them. They are very serious about their new business and wanted to start right with no setbacks.

"I'm sorry it's not the news you wanted, but I have to be realistic with you. I don't want to lead you in the wrong direction by giving you something you can't afford. Some other mortgage guy may give you something that they know you can't manage. But I am an honest man and I do care about every one of my clients. My business has grown because of my honesty and my care, which is something that is lacking in this industry. I can give you some referrals to ease your mind. I am willing to work with you throughout your mortgage process. So if you have any additional future investment plans, I would work with you to fulfill this goal. Just trust me." Harry pitched with sincerity. Laverne and Barney was more than convinced that Harry would be their mortgage guy. They just had to start very small.

Laverne and Barney worked with their real estate agent. Unfortunately, because of the low loan they qualified for they were only able to view in certain neighborhoods. They viewed neighborhoods that they did not prefer and that weren't a part of their plan. It wasn't a culturally mixed and upcoming neighborhood. Instead it was a neighborhood that was very challenging and with difficulty to rent at market.

Harry called his other clients, Martella and Maurice, who were averaging an income of $150,000 and fair to good credit. He told them that with a lot of hard work on his part, that he was able to find a loan for them that would put them in their ideal investment neighborhood. They were extremely happy to hear that they would be able to qualify for a prime investment property with their qualification. Martella and Maurice were able to purchase an investment property that rented above market with a better than great investment return.

Martella and Maurice were both British and were able to invest in a predominately white neighborhood. While, Laverne and Barney were both Mexican and they were able to invest in a predominately Hispanic neighborhood.

The Test

Butch has been in the mortgage business for many years. He hasn't been very successful as he had wanted. His business is situated in a culturally mixed neighborhood. It was once a predominately white affluent neighborhood. He thought that a lot of lower income people had moved in due to the affordable housing campaign that the government instituted. His plans of retiring with an easy lifestyle went down the tubes.

Tatiana, a single, heavy set mother of two children wanted to know how much she qualified for a new home. She had saved throughout the years and was given a gift from her mother to help with the down payment. After doing some on-line research, she learned that she have enough for a 30% down payment for houses in her desired neighborhood. She wanted to move into a better neighborhood with a better school district for her children. She did an on line mortgage application where she was able to qualify for her desired homes, but decided to visit Butch to meet face to face with a mortgage person.

Butch knew that Tatiana was qualified for her desired home, but was very disgruntle. He was very resentful that someone like Tatiana can afford a better home than the one he had.

What should he do?

1. Give her a balloon mortgage to entice her with the initial low mortgage payments and a later surprise, unbearable payments. This way she will lose her home and move back to her old neighborhood.
2. Give her a fixed low rate mortgage with comfortable payments where she would be able to continue saving and improve her lifestyle. In this case he would wish her good luck in purchasing her dream home and mumble to himself how much he hates her.
3. Give her a low mortgage amount, where she couldn't purchase in her desired neighborhood. Explain to her that the on line mortgage companies will tell her the same thing and that he is true to his word.

Chapter 11

Steering

The Scenario

Have you ever heard someone say "this place suits you", while looking for a home? When they really mean you're around your own race. Have you ever walked into a store and the sales person immediately starts following you around, asking if you need help? When they really mean, can they help you out of their store. Have you ever gone shopping, and you are constantly told that the item is pretty expensive. When they really mean that you should try shopping somewhere else, because you can't afford it. This is how people steer you in the direction that they want you to take and NOT the direction that you want to take.

Shelley had just got custody of her niece, Pamela. Unfortunately, Pamela's parents had recently passed after getting into a car accident. In their will, they left Pamela in Shelley's care. Shelley wanted to get a new home for them both, where Pamela would be happy. After searching on-line for quite some time, she thought it would be easier for someone else to do the work. One day she went to Blue Sky Realty. A very friendly agent interviewed her to get her wants and needs.

Shelley stated that an absolute must should be 1) family

friendly neighborhood, 2) great school area, 3) park nearby. Her agent Pauline said, "Oh, that's an easy list. I'm sure I will be able to find what you need". She also wanted a small house, two bedrooms, two bathrooms, and a fenced in yard, which was move in ready. Pauline went to work immediately. Pauline thought it would be a challenge to satisfy Shelley, but didn't want to say anything that she wasn't supposed to say. As she went through the available office listing, she just couldn't find anything that she thought would be right for Shelley. Although she normally prefers to stay with the office listings, she felt that she had no choice but to use the MLS for other listings. The MLS had a broader listing base.

Shelley decided to call Pauline, "Hey, Pauline. I was looking on-line and saw a few homes I wanted to look at. Can I email you the information?"

"Sure, or if you have the MLS number you can just give it to me now." Pauline said.

"OK," Shelley said. She gave Pauline the MLS numbers and then emailed the additional information. She was confident that one of the homes would be a perfect fit for them.

Pauline looked at the homes that Shelley had given her and thought that it was crazy for her to pick them. One of the homes was a 3 bedroom, 2 bathrooms, in an expensive city area near a very active night life. The second home was a 1 bedroom, 1 1/2 bath, with a den and a finished basement. It was in an area where Pauline thought was too rural and far from the central businesses. The third home was a beautifully designed new home, 4 bedroom, 3 1/2 bathrooms, 2500 square footage, and all new everything. Pauline thought it was too much of a house for Shelley and was in the hills near a park trail. She disregarded all three suggestions and continued to look sincerely for Shelley.

Pauline scheduled four homes for her to view over the weekend. Shelley was very excited and was ready and eager to buy a home immediately. They met at the first home. It was on a cul-de-sac, mature community, and quiet neighborhood. Shelley saw two children playing down the street. Her niece was tagging along. The house was a ranch style, 2 bedrooms, 1 1/2 bathroom, and an unfinished basement. "I don't know if this house is right for Pamela. It seems too quiet."

"I know it appears that way but there are a couple of kids on the street. And the neighborhood is pretty. You can look up the statistics for the crime rate. You won't be disappointed. It's a good resting place." Pauline said.

"Resting place?" Shelley asked.

"I mean you won't have any problem here. The people here are friendly and experienced." Pauline assured her.

The second home is near a park in a gated community. It was a condo, 2 bedroom, 2 1/2 bathroom and assigned parking. It had a community pool, gym, community park. "Now, this place is perfect for you. It has everything in your must list. You'll love it." Pauline said.

"Yeah, but it's not a house. I thought we were looking at houses. I thought that was understood." Shelley said.

"Well. This is just as good. You'll see. Just give it a chance." Shelley couldn't stand the condo and wasn't satisfied with anything. They went to see the third house.

They pulled up to a Tudor home. Finally, Shelly thought, a house worth seeing. It was in a heavily populated Italian community.

"Well. This is a three bedroom, so you can use one for an office. Two and a half bathroom, one is an en-suite. A very good size family area for entertaining during the holidays. Plenty of room for when the family comes over to visit." Pauline walked her around pointing out the unique details of the house. Shelley was awed by it and soon fell in love. The basement was semi-finished and there was plenty of storage area.

"I think I like this one." Shelley said. "But what about the homes that I sent you?"

"Oh, those. They were... already had offers. Sorry. I meant to tell you earlier, but I got so wrapped up in trying to find the right home for you." Pauline lied.

"Oh." Shelley said.

"So, do you want to see the last house? Or do you want to make an offer on this one?"

"Well, let's see the last house. But I do love this one."

"OK." Pauline headed toward the fourth home. The fourth home was an older home that had a lot of charm. It was in a very quiet neighborhood. It was a small house approximately 1300 square feet living space. A two bedroom, 1 1/2 bathrooms, and laundry room on the main floor. Pauline thought that it would be perfect for Shelley. It was small enough for her to manage and in a safe neighborhood.

"It's quaint. But I don't think I want this neighborhood. I don't think it's right for Pamela." Shelley said.

"Pamela? Oh, she would love it. This is a perfect home.

She can play outside in the backyard and you won't have to worry about the safety."

"Well, I'm more concerned about her making friends. She is going to move into a new community where she would need to make friends easily. It doesn't seem that this neighborhood have any children. It's not near a park. It's seems boring for her." Shelley insisted.

"No. That's not true. Why don't you look up the statistics on this area? You'll find that it confirms what you are looking for. You'll see. Don't you want to be in a safe neighborhood? Somewhere you are comfortable. The people here, you will find, to have similar interests." Pauline said.

"What?"

"Well, your family would adjust perfectly. You'll see. I would consider this one too." Pauline said.

Shelley was reflecting on her day as she sat down to watch television. After she thought about the events, she thought that Pauline was being pretty discriminatory. Yes, she was an older Italian single lady who had just gained custody of her grandniece, but she should not have been treated in the manner that Pauline treated her. She kind of felt that Pauline thought she was about to die from old age and that she had to live in a quiet, Italian, low maintenance neighborhood. She thought that Pauline didn't even consider the fact that Pamela was in the picture and that she wanted a right fit for her niece.

The Test

As an agent, your broker gives you a new client to work with. They are a couple of seniors who just came from Jamaica to live closer to their children in the United States. Unfortunately, their children had no space for them in their home. The husband had significant health problems and was on an oxygen machine. They wanted a home close to their family, preferably in walking distance. They had limited fixed income.

Which home would you want them in?

- o **Home 1**: In walking distance to their family. 1 bedroom, 1 bathroom, condo on first floor. No elevator. Predominately black neighborhood. Priced slightly over their budget with

no room for negotiation.
- *Home 2*: 15 minutes from their family. Predominately white neighborhood. Studio apartment. Half the cost of their budget. No parking. Elevator building with amenities on site.
- *Home 3*: 30 minutes from their family. Mixed neighborhood. Walking distance from the hospital and the park. Elevator building. Coop and within their budget. Board approval is difficult and there is a waiting list.
- *Home 4*: short distance from their family. Noisy neighborhood with lots of activities. High income area. Predominately Jewish community. Near prestigious college. Near private nursing home. One bedroom apartment for rent in a multi-family home within their budget. One hour away from major hospital. Known community to have burglaries.
- *Home 5*: short distance from their family. Predominately Caribbean neighborhood. Small shops in downtown market area. 1 bedroom apartment in small elevator building. On budget and short distance from local hospital.

Chapter 12

Blockbusting

The Scenario

Picture this, a small town consisting of predominantly white neighborhood. The breakdown of the demographics is 89% White, 5% Black, and 6% Asian in Town of Lichter. Kassandra wanted to purchase a home in a racially mixed neighborhood. Power House Realty agent, Melissa, desperately needed to build her clientele and to secure listings. Kassandra went to Power House Realty to inquire about finding a home. Power House Realty is located in Lichter. Melissa introduced herself and brought Kassandra to a room where they can discuss her wish list for her new home. Melissa and Kassandra discussed her pre-approved loan, where she was not qualified to get the house with all her criteria. Her price range did not get her the 3000 square footage she wanted or the pool she feels she needs. Melissa shows her various homes that were on the market in her price range. Kassandra gets frustrated and said she will see if she can qualify for a bigger loan, which would allow her to purchase the home that fits her checklist.

The next day Melissa gets Kassandra's new pre-approval loan for an increased amount. Melissa can't believe her eyes and doesn't know how Kassandra did it, but she has to accept the pre-approval as a valid document. Melissa discusses Kassandra's case with her broker, Janice. Janice asks Melissa about how successful is she going to be, if she tries to put Kassandra in the neighborhood she had chosen during her meeting. Melissa gets nervous about keeping Kassandra as her client and prefers to move on, but figures that she will try to get some listing out of this impossible task.

Melissa knows a few people in Kassandra's desired neighborhood. She tells them that some real estate office is trying to go politically correct by introducing some blacks into the neighborhood, so that they can grow their business and increase their market share. She also tells them that the government has been cracking down on agency's who are not acting ethically. These people grow alarmed that some Realtors are going to rent or sell homes to blacks in their neighborhood. A false rumor spreads that Power House has begun to sell homes to blacks in the neighborhood and for at market price, instead of the trended above market price. Some of the neighbors decided to contact Melissa to list their homes to secure an above market price and to leave the dreaded area where blacks were to populate.

Melissa secures five listings, two at the market price, and three at above market price. Melissa, unsuccessfully, was not able to secure Kassandra a house due to offer and acceptance disagreements. She sells the two houses that were listed at market to two young white couples. She sells one of the above market houses to an Asian couple. After some time the neighbors do not see any black homeowners in their affluent part of the neighborhood, so their panic subsided. Power House Realty grew its reputation to comply with their affluent neighborhood's demands and was able to shake off the government, as the rumor was told.

The Test

You are a new agent.

Your race is white.

You work for an agency that is located in a predominately Hispanic neighborhood.

The agents at your agency are predominately Hispanic.

Your broker wants you to prove yourself and requires that new agents produce at least 3 listing a month.

Your broker provides little to no in-house training and requires that you take additional training on your own through the local Realtor association.

Your financial situation does not support the ability to gain training through the Realtor association's high price.

It is three weeks into your first month without any listing.

The broker constantly reminds you that you must secure three listings before months end, because he doesn't want unproductive agents and that he is running a business.

What do you do?
1. Find another agency that is racially in your favor.
2. File a discrimination suit against the realty for unfair treatment.
3. Introduce your bilingual self to the neighborhood and falsely state you are from a Hispanic country. Then tell them discreetly that a pro-white, republican organization is establishing their political headquarters in the neighborhood in order to move in and take over businesses. In addition, tell them the group will have a great political influence in the government that would eventually raise taxes, which would increase rents.
4. Send out a just sold mailing depicting a black couple owning a near-by home to various different locations in the region, where it implies that blacks are moving in the neighborhood.
5. Speak to your broker to find a solution to your listing issues.

PART FOUR

The Contract

Chapter 13

Before

Equal Opportunity

    As a real estate agent, engaging in the sale process is important because it involves different forms of agreements and contracts that should contain important, factual, and accurate information. Members of the contract must sign to the agreement, so no errors should be made. It is a life changing event. Mortgages, deeds, ownership establishment, other financial obligations, and legal rights are all outlined in the contract. This is one reason why real estate agents are classified as professionals and not as employees. There are legal, ethical and contractual responsibilities that they must adhere to.

    In the United States, there are numerous types of people living together under one nation. We need to understand one another better in order to live in peace. Throughout the years many people have immigrated to this country in order to have a better life. They wanted that American dream. They wanted the ability to one day own their own home with a white picket fence and the independence and freedoms that they were told were attainable. The American dream, though, involved the American culture. It is important for everyone to understand that the culture they immigrated from is different in some way from the American culture. The American dream was designed for everyone with the understanding that rules and laws had to be followed to obtain this dream.

Because people immigrated from various parts of the world, they brought a part of their culture and ideology to United States. In some respect they integrated their culture with the American culture. But what is the American culture? To define this would be introducing a debate. For the American culture has various cultures mixed in, where the ones that are generally accepted is integrated. America is a country where they promote respect for all cultures, whether we accept them are not. With this concept, what is not generally accepted may still exist in this country.

People with different cultures and backgrounds want the same opportunities, so they can achieve their goals. No one should be refused that opportunity based on who they are or what they are. Unfortunately, not everyone feels this way, which is why we still have discrimination. The laws have changed extending the protective classes of people forbidding discrimination. There are some people who feel they should also add protection to people with a specific bloodline. For example, just because you are a descendant of a known historical criminal, doesn't mean that you are or that you should be treated like one. I'm sure his descendants don't want to be discriminated against. I'm sure that nearly everyone had someone in their bloodline that had did something wrong; whether it is from war or from crime or for survival.

The fact is that discrimination stems in the minds of the people of what they are willing to accept. It stems from fear that a particular class of people may violate their needs or their own wants. It stems from the feeling of "those people" are different and shouldn't be mixed with my kind. It stems from the underlying fact that to accept what they do not feel comfortable with will somehow change their own person hood and identity. Whatever it may be, it is wrong; because discrimination involves action against someone and not just the thought of not accepting someone. When we take action against someone for not accepting them, we have committed an injustice. We then have taken the rights and freedoms away from someone; the very rights and freedoms we wish no one will take from us.

The anti-discrimination law has a protective class of people as follows:
1. Race
2. Color

3. Religion
4. National origin
5. Age
6. Sex
7. Pregnancy
8. Citizenship
9. Familial status
10. Disability status
11. Veteran status
12. Genetic information

Ready Willing and Able Buyer

As an agent you will be dealing with a lot more buyers than sellers. These buyers sometimes consume your time irresponsibly. They may just be looking for fun. It's hard to believe but some people have a profession of viewing homes for their simple enjoyment. Of course, this will not be the norm. An experienced agent will have a procedure in obtaining worthy buyers. How do you identify worthy buyers? Well, you know not to rely on promises that they will get a loan pre-approval. Don't waste your time if they don't even have one. They may not qualify for the houses you plan to show them. A pre-approval may indicate that the buyer has some down payment and what they are financially capable of affording.

If the buyer is unsure that they are willing to purchase a home at this time, then you shouldn't waste your time showing them properties. You should focus on buyers who are looking for purchasing *now*. Buyers now a days can search on the Internet for what they may want in their future, on their own time. It shouldn't be your job to be their friend and provide them with what-if's scenarios of potential purchases.

Sometimes you may find the perfect property for your buyer, but they are not willing to accept the terms of the agreement. In such as case, they should not be forced to proceed. The last thing you need is for them to accuse you of coercion in purchasing a property that they are not 100% sure about. They need to be absolutely sure that it is the right home for them. It is not OK to just satisfy their checklist. They must feel that they will enjoy the home.

Market Analysis

Market analysis is a tool to determine the current value of a property. It's an important tool. Wouldn't you want to know if a listing is overpriced or underpriced? Wouldn't you want to know how a listing is faired in a particular area? Market analysis is essential in the negotiating process. You also must consider location, type of home, time on the market, and other variables when it comes to valuing a property. A good market analysis would include these variables. An area 10 years ago may market a home at $200,000 but today it is marketed at $500,000. Many things may have happened in ten years. A prestigious private school may have been built in the area. More business may have entered the area. The average mean income may have gone up. The home itself may have had improvements that brought up its value. When a market analysis is done, it compares similar properties in the area to value the property for sale. Comparable properties should be very close to the components of the for sale property. Therefore, you shouldn't compare a three bedroom single family home with a two family home. You shouldn't compare a 1500 sq ft ranch style home to a 2500 sq ft Tudor home. They are too different for comparisons.

Chapter 14

During

Offer and Acceptance

      The most important part in purchasing your home is the offer and acceptance. It is where it could become very exciting and sometimes very emotional. For first time home buyers it may be more emotional than anything else. It is a dream comes true. On the other hand, it shows the skills of the negotiating agents. The buyer agent must fairly represent their buyers. They should negotiate an offer that the buyers agree to. This would mean to do a market analysis to see what the property is valued at and compare it with what the owner is selling it for. If it is overpriced, then there should be some negotiation in getting a good price for your buyers. In addition if there are work to be done on the home, that also can be negotiated to reflect a lower price. Many other reasons may cause a negotiation, such as seller relocating or an estate sale. Whatever the reason, it is your obligation to work hard to get the best price for your buyer.

      On the flip side, if you are representing the seller, you should try to get the best and highest price. You may suggest staging the property to be sold. You should communicate with the seller of any necessary maintenance that should be done to prevent bringing the property value down. The property must be presented to yield the greatest value. You may recommend the seller to do an inspection to avoid any surprise negotiation that may occur from the buyers' inspection. If the seller is prepared for any possibility of a low offer, it would be in their best interest to have the tools to support their counteroffer. In contrast, sellers may be presented with a bidding war. In such a case the sellers' agent should take the initiative to provide the seller with the necessary information about the readiness of each buyer.

Once an acceptance is given, there is relief on both sides and hopefully a seamless transaction well done. Remember dotting your I's and crossing your T's are important in every legal transaction, so make sure your paperwork is correct.

Counteroffer

Counteroffer occurs when the seller does not agree with the buyers offer. Some buyers refuse to put in an offer above their budget no matter what the property is selling for. In such a case, a counteroffer may not bring them to increase their initial offer. Other buyers may want to just start low to see how flexible the seller is willing to go; but this is risky. If they start too low, it may be insulting to the seller where they would not even entertain that buyer. The agent should consult with sincerity of how important an offer is and to put in an offer that is respectably negotiable.

In addition to putting in a good offer, the agent should confirm the buyer's documents are accurate and viable. The last thing you need as an agent is that the documents are not current and the buyer's financial situation has changed where they are no longer capable of making the purchase. It takes time to find a property so changes can occur while you are in the process of their search. If indeed their financial information has changed, then it may give way to present a better offer or a lower offer. Therefore, the counteroffer may also change in accordance. Note that the seller's position may also change which can also affect the counteroffer. Always keep up to date with your client's position.

Inspection: Radon Gas

In the inspection process it is important to identify all matters that must be addressed before buying a home. You do not want to find out after the fact. The information may be valuable in negotiating the price with the sellers. The sellers may also fix the problems prior to the purchase, which will alleviate any burden on the buyers. The most important matters that buyers should consider are radon gas, lead base paint, and asbestos.

Radon gas is odorless and cannot be detected by sight. It is a radioactive gas. People can get a radon detector kit to test for it. It's the only means of knowing if you are being exposed to this gas. It can slowly kill you if you are not aware of it. Although there are ways you can address the matter yourself, it is best to properly treat it by hiring a professional. Radon gas can cause very serious health effects, such as cancer.

Inspection: Lead Base Paint Disclosure

The lead base paint disclosure is required in the real estate industry. You should provide this disclosure to any potential buyer. If lead base paint is known to exist in the home, it should be disclosed in writing with proper signatures. Lead is an element that can cause health problems in many people. Particularly children can fall prey to it, by simply playing around the metal and eating paint chips. It can cause damage to some organs and contaminate your blood. It is said that it leads to learning disabilities along with other behavioral problems. It is wise to avoid contact to this element and to have knowledge of its existence. Some older homes may have lead base paint. Moreover, lead can be in other building materials such as tiles. A professional lead test is recommended, especially in cases where you may have home improvement projects that you are doing yourself. Being careful is being knowledgeable.

Inspection: Asbestos

Asbestos is a material used in building products that causes serious health problems. It was once used as durable insulation in many homes. At the time, they did not know the health problems that would occur from exposure to this product. It is known to have caused problems to the people who worked with the product and family members who were around the workers. The fibers inhaled stays in your system and are difficult to come out. It can build up and cause a known health cancer called Mesothelioma.

Now, homes with asbestos in them should be professional addressed. They can either remove the asbestos or contain it so that it doesn't cause health conditions. It is advised to have it removed.

Encroachment/Easements

It should be disclosed whether the property you are selling has any encroachment. Encroachment is when the property line has been occupied by another or by something. To avoid this, property line should be clearly marked or staked. Any disputable encroachment can be hopefully, successfully, addressed with a proven outline of the property called a survey.

Encroachments may occur when a building extends their addition across their property line. It occurs when a fence is put up incorrectly on your property. Another example is a shared driveway, where one leaves their equipment on your side of the property. Respecting boundaries is recommended for keeping a good relationship with neighborhoods. It keeps you out of court. If you do have to go to court to resolve any issues, it is good to have adequate proof of where your property lines are. You should communicate with the encroacher, and show that you attempted to address the issue in a timely manner. Procrastinating may cause additional problems. You should use due diligence in any conflict.

Certificate of Occupancy

Certificate of occupancy is a document given to establish the confirmation that a dwelling is habitable. If there are improvements, renovations, additions, and areas in the home that are questionable; it is advisable to get a certificate of occupancy from the local government. If you are trying to sell your home and a pre-existing addition is present, but you are unsure that it was a legal addition, it is advised that you check your building department to clarify anything that is disputable. Some people may turn a single family home into a multifamily home without proper permits. Renovations such as an added room may not have the proper approval. There are basements that have been turned into a rental, which may not have the proper clearance from your local building office. A general rule is that anything that appears to be questionable should be checked with the building department. Rules, regulations, and codes changes as laws changes; which may have an impact on the certificate of occupancy; so it is a smart idea to keep up to date with them. It, also, provides that the dwelling is presumably safe.

In some cases, homes may have to be put back in the state prior to renovations to establish a legal occupancy. In other cases, you may have to pay fees to bring it up to code. No matter what, you cannot sell a property without a valid certificate of occupancy. It is normally the burden of the seller.

Chapter 15

Final

Title & Deeds

A title is a document outlining who owns the property. During the closing, the title company should have their representatives present. They should already have done their work in verifying the accuracy of who owns the property free and clear. There may be liens on the property, and it is the job of the title company to identify any liens on the property. Liens are when the property owner has financial obligations to someone and they can take part ownership until that obligation is satisfied. Liens should be addressed prior to selling the property. Unless you plan to agree on satisfying the liens of the sellers, the property should be free and clear of any liens. The title company then can establish new ownership with the buyer free of any liens on the document.

The title should have the old owners and the new owners in print and signed by all parties. There may be times that the title has a seller's name that wasn't presented to the buyer during the sales process. Although, this should never occur, it simply means that someone else has been appointed to sell the property in the seller's absence. Nevertheless, the owner of the property must be indicated on the title document for it to be valid. The title will be passed on to the buyer during the closing process and is proof of the new ownership.

Closing Cost

It is now closing day where the buyer has to be ready to make the payment for the home. They must be prepared to make out several checks to satisfy the closing costs. Some of the costs include, but not limited to:
- Origination fee
- Discount points
- PMI (private mortgage insurance)
- Title services (insurance)
- Escrow
- Appraisal fees
- Taxes
- Attorney fees
- Homeowners insurance
- Survey fees
- Processing fee
- Underwriting fee

Be prepared to sign documents in duplicates. The buyer should have already put a down payment on the property to secure the home and show that they are serious in purchasing it.

Most fees are important and necessary, but there may be added fees that are specific to your type of purchase. Buying a condo or a co-op may have other fees specific to them.

Once the closing is over, you will be given the key to the home. From that point it is officially your home.

PART FIVE

Home Responsibilities

Chapter 16

Property Value

Types of Loans

From the perspective of the homeowner, we can see how owning a real estate redefines your future. You are no longer renting, every bit of your money does not go to your landlord. Your property is now your investment. Your home is now building value. You have the freedom to improve upon your home and make it your own. You have the power to decorate without worrying that you are damaging the property. You can hammer into the wall if you want. You can change that sink if you want. You can come home late at night without worrying about disturbing your neighbors. You can add sophisticated security if you want. Simply, there is much more freedom of owning than renting.

The value of your property depends on factors that affect your finances. Your property value is dependent on the location, the market, the type of property, and if you owe any loans on it. If you try to sell your property with loans or liens, it can significantly devalue your home. Building equity is necessary to offset the expenses on your property. Therefore, loans and liens need to be addressed pro-actively.

The two main mortgage loans are fixed and adjustable rate mortgages. Having a mortgage is a big responsibility. You should know what you are getting into before signing documents.

Unfortunately, lots of people don't know what the mortgage entails. They depend on what is explained to them by lenders. The language that is written on loan documents is strategically designed for bankers and lawyers. Everyday people, normally, will not understand the details of a mortgage. Moreover, the mortgage documents are pages and pages of legal documents. The adjustable loan mortgage may be written in a crafty manner. It is extremely advisable to seek professional assistance in understanding your mortgage prior to signing any documents.

A fixed rate mortgage is where the interest rate is fixed for a specified time frame. Your monthly mortgage payment will not increase for the duration of the loan. Most people prefer this type of mortgage because their payments are locked in where there are no surprises. The owners may feel more secure with this loan. Your lender will qualify you based on your down payment and credit history. It is possible that you may not qualify for the loan amount that you requested. The lender will indicate to you what amount you can afford based on your individual circumstances. Loan period can be 10, 15, 20, or 30 years. Most people have a 30 year mortgage. People that have a shorter year term may be using the mortgage for investment purposes, where they plan to sell their property and not live in it. Your interest rate will depend on your credit worthiness. People that have better than normal credit will often time get a lower rate than someone who has a fair credit history. One fixed mortgage that you should watch out for is balloon mortgages. Balloon mortgages start out very low because you are paying a smaller amount of the interest on the loan initially. But you must be ready to pay the balloon portion of the loan when it is due. Some people run into problems trying to pay the balloon portion, so be careful with this one.

An adjustable rate mortgage (ARM) is where the interest changes with the market. There is a margin (base) rate and an index (fluctuating rate that depends on the market). It is possible that every year the rate may change where your monthly payment changes as well. There are different types of ARM's where it may start out fixed for a specified time period and then change. What's best for you depends on how you plan to use the property. This is a risky mortgage because you just don't know what the market may bring.

In some cases, banks do not mind if the owner prepays their loans to shorten their years. However, prepaying will not decrease the amount owed. It will bring equity into your home faster. You can take out additional loans based on your equity for home improvement projects or for various other things. With this noted, you should be cautious that you don't become house poor where you are bombarded with too much loans and too much projects and expenses.

Making Payments

A reasonable scenario is to have a mortgage payment that does not exceed more than half of your take home pay. If you cannot put aside any money to save, you are not in a good financial situation. Having a mortgage should not replace your ability to save. You can indicate how to distribute your payment if you choose to pay more than your monthly requirement. Some people like to make an extra payment every year by apply this payment towards their principal amount. Therefore, it will be reducing the principal balance in the long run. On your monthly statement, some lenders provide detail information. If you have an escrow with your lender, you should see when they pay the taxes or any other local required payments. In some cases, homeowners insurance is paid through your lender. During tax time, the lender should provide tax documents, form 1098, for you to use on filing your taxes. In addition to this form, you should also keep any receipts for any home improvements and maintenance to your property. These documents may be used to offset taxes due.

Your monthly mortgage payments should always be on time. If you fall late on payments, the bank may charge fees and eventually may foreclose on your property. During these days, we have lived through an historical mortgage crisis. Many people have lost their homes due to predator lending. In a foreclosure process, banks take the homes from the owner and put it back on the market to recoup what is owed to them. So, a bank can sell your home for $20,000 if that is what is owed to them, no matter if you mortgaged your property over that amount. You will then be without your property. If it is possible to work out an agreement with your bank to reestablish trust, it is advisable that you do so. You should make every effort to keep your home. In the case where you may need assistance in doing so, there are HUD organizations that may pose as intermediaries. You can also seek advice from your attorney.

As a basic understanding what happens in the real estate

market affects the economy. If there is an historical, detrimental amount of foreclosures in the society, it can cause a catastrophically impact on the economy. This is what happened in the United States. A simple reason is that the bank is directly connected to the real estate industry and other important industries. The banking system is not independent of any industry, so the crisis has a domino effect through society. New laws and changes to the banking industry have helped to pacify the crisis at hand. Unfortunately, there is no fool proof solution to this crisis, and there may be loop holes that can cause another catastrophe. You should keep in mind how to handle your personal financial situation and take any necessary steps in securing your financial future. Therefore, don't take more than you can handle.

Liens

Property liens vary and can force a homeowner out of their home. Contractors can put a lien on your home if you fail to pay for their work. Unpaid property taxes can cause liens on your home, as well. Unpaid water bills can cause a lien. Judgments for unpaid child support can create a lien on your property. Liens are judgment debts that are put on your home. You must satisfy the debt in order to legally remove the liens.

To avoid liens you should review contractual agreements carefully and make sure that all parties fulfill their agreements. Sometimes disputes may occur when contractors do not adequately satisfy the owner. In which, the owner may refuse to pay for the service. This may prompt the contractor to take out a judgment against the property owner. Where there is a dispute in service, it may be advisable to satisfy the debt and then seek legal action. Construction liens are sometimes called mechanical liens. These types of liens, if possible, should be avoided. You wouldn't want to pay legal fees for something that could be remedied. But if you've exhausted all efforts, then any disputes should be addressed in court.

Increase property taxes may prevent homeowners from paying their taxes. Taxes must be paid in full at the time it is due. Since they must be paid in full, some homeowners fall short on payment and just cannot afford to pay. Penalties may be imposed by your local government on top of what is owed, which further exasperate the problem. The burden of having an accumulated debt causes a lien to be imposed on homeowners. If it is easier to have an escrow established through your lender, it may be advisable to do so. This would alleviate the stress of being prepared to paying the entire property taxes. Your lender can do it for you through escrow.

Chapter 17

Maintenance & Upgrade

Maintenance

    Enjoying your home can be more fun if it's not falling apart. If you didn't buy a fixer upper, you should not have to put too much effort in maintaining your home. Keeping up your home is one of the responsibilities of being a homeowner; not keeping up with your neighbors.

    Maintaining your home is not the same as making improvements. It's important to know the difference when it comes to tax time. Certain changes you make in your home may have tax benefits. Any changes you make should be considered when valuing your home. You do not want to make changes that will decrease the value of your home. Some maintenance work is as follows.

    Chimney cleaning should be routine, especially if there is a functioning fireplace. But if you do not have a fireplace, it still should be cleaned of any debris buildup. Due to weather conditions, your chimney may need minor repairs. If you get a routine chimney clean, your worker should indicate to you if there are repairs needed.

    Landscape work can be very involved depending on your desires. It also can be very expensive. Adding trees and shrubs can put a dent in your pocket if you have a large property. Removing them can be equally expensive. Sometimes overgrown trees can be hazardous during bad weather. Fences should be repaired or painted to keep rust from forming and to prevent natural wear and tear. Pressure washing your exterior to your home would make your home look cleaner and brand new. Mowing your lawn should be a regular thing. You should not be the only person in your neighborhood with an overgrown lawn. Overgrown lawn can make people think the house is abandoned or that you are on vacation. Masonry work should be kept up to date. Bricks, walkways, and plaster deteriorate overtime. It wouldn't be recommended that you keep dated outdoor furniture. You may have spent a lot of money for the furniture when it was in style, but if it is furniture that is cheap or looks dated you should replace it. A dated house can bring down the value.

Depending upon the age of your home, you should have an electrician evaluate your wiring. This could be very important, because codes and laws change, and it may be safer to rewire and upgrade. Another important one is plumbing. Every homeowner will experience some plumbing issues during their ownership. Plumbing problems should be taken care of immediately; delaying repairs can be disastrous. A little water damage can cause a huge problem. If you have carpet and pets, carpet cleaning is a must. Pet hair, fleas, dusts and unsightly critters may be in the carpet. People normally paint to change the appearance of the area, but painting should be more than sprucing up. Paint gets dirty, dull, and dated. Periodic painting, to put forth newness to the home, is recommended. For style purposes, decor should be changed with the times. To reiterate, unless you have an historical home, anything that dates your home brings down the value. A dirty home is an unwanted home, so everyday cleaning should be a requirement. A thorough "spring cleaning" should be done at least once a year. Don't be a hoarder. Sometimes space is an issue, repositioning your decor can make improvements to this problem. Starter homes would most often come with space issues. You may want to consider purchasing a bigger home when you have outgrown a starter home.

Upgrade

Upgrades are improvements that increase the value of your home, sometimes considerably based on the type of improvements. You can purchase a home for $300,000 and have improvement costs of $20,000; where the new market value could show an immediate increase of $370,000. Over time it can even increase considerably more, depending on the location and condition. Some improvements may come with warranty, which can be an important piece of document when you eventually sell your home. It reassures the buyer of an expense that they do not have to incur.

Replacing or repairing your roof should be on the top of your list. If there are any damages to the roof it may cause other damages to the home. When repairing your roof, you may want to check out your gutters as well. Gutters help the rain water run off away from your home. You do not want any water buildup into your home or near your home foundation. Always keep you gutters free from debris and leaves. Make any necessary repairs to leakage. Windows is another major improvement that should be upgraded when necessary. Windows are part of insulation for your home. Saving energy should also be on your mind when making improvements. Living in an urban environment may make people not conscious of the value of saving energy and saving the environment. Every effort should be made to recapture saving the environment.

Expanding your space, may require permits from your local government. Adding additional living space will definitely increase your home value. Your overall expense should be considered an investment. If you have space to add a garage, it would be a plus. Garages are used for storing your cars, but most importantly used for storage. Storage space is almost always demanded in every home. Everyone loves a finished basement. Adding a finished basement gives room for recreational activities, rentals, office, and other miscellaneous uses. Some people use it as a dedicated business area, where they can outline clearly their square footage on their tax returns. Some people may also use it as a dedicated escape space away from the family, i.e. man cave. Having an outdoor living space, such as a back porch is also a bonus. Barbecues are part of an American tradition. Also more people are buying hot tubs for entertaining. These outdoor additions are in an increasing demand. The two most important selling features in a home is the bathroom and the kitchen. Old appliances should be replaced with newer energy efficient appliances. It would add even more value to your home if you can replace them with state of the art appliances. These types of appliances last longer and keep their value. Counter tops and cabinets provides a greater look and style to your home. Dated cabinets should be refaced or replaced. Bathrooms tend to reveal the personality of the owners. They may be shower only people or spa like people or elderly people, where railings are needed. Whatever your needs are or your style, you should keep up with the renovations. Tiles always need up keeping and proper cleaning. Last but not least are the floors. Wood floors can get damaged throughout the years. If pieces of your wood floor can be replaced with a perfect match, it should be. Otherwise replacing the entire floor can be costly, but a wise move.

Chapter 18

Using Your Home

Quiet Enjoyment

Where you live and what kind of personality you have makes a difference in what kind of enjoyment you get out of your home. Whether you live in the city, suburb, or country; the demands of these environment will have an impact on your livelihood. These environments have different school structure, different transportation, promote different types of business structures, and may harness a different type of culture or language. If you define quiet enjoyment as no loud noise when you go to bed, compared to no loud noise during the day; then living in the city or the suburb may be for you. If you prefer quietness all the time; then you should lean more to the suburb or the country. Quiet enjoyment just does not mean noise, but also no pestering or harassment by anyone. To be in peace in your home is sometimes difficult, especially if in your home you have family or friends that may take that away from you.

Most cities now have laws regarding noise. The blowing of car horns unnecessarily may not be permitted. Yelling at night may not be permitted. Now a days, people may call the police when these things occur, so that they can get peacefulness. People use their backyard, their porch, or their balcony as the place of quiet enjoyment. Watching nature, the people, and the city life provides their minds to relax. Relaxation comes with feeling safe. Some people feel safe around lots of people. They prefer not to be alone or isolated. While other people feel safer with less people around them; the lack of people ensures a more predictable environment. Your personality will set the demands of the location of where you want to live. Outside of this, the type of home you have also constitutes enjoyment.

Quiet enjoyment may not come to you in a small home compared to if you have a larger more spacious home. If you have nowhere to go for peace and quiet in your home, no matter what location you are in; there will be no quiet enjoyment. Home provides a sort of safety net or an escape for some. If you outgrow your home, you may find it very difficult to locate that escape area in it. People use various rooms for that escape such as their study, their walk up attic space, their basement, their garage, or even their bedroom. It is that one place where you can remove yourself from activities or from disruptions in your daily life. It is to sit down, to lie down and to think. It is to do your hobby and concentrate. The escape of the very routine, of the very demanding, of the very burdensome things; would be your enjoyment. Yet, some people leave their home to find this enjoyment. They go to their religious place of worship. Some people just won't live far away from their place of worship; so that culture places an important part in getting your quiet enjoyment and buying your home in that perfect location.

Where ever and however you find your quiet enjoyment is up to you. But sometimes it may cost you dearly. You may have to pay for that expensive home on the side of the city that will give you that enjoyment. You may have to buy a bigger home than you really need to get that satisfaction out of your home. Keep in mind that your wants, needs, and desires come with a price.

Investors

For the people who do not wish to enjoy their home they bought, they may look more to having it as an investment. To some they flip homes; to others they get a rental stream out of it. Homes that are "flipped" are bought for below market value, renovated, and then sold again for a profit. Homes that are for rental properties, are bought at a competitive price, renovated for rental purposes, and then rented to produce a profit. Investors do not want to lose money in these types of properties, but sometimes it happens.

Flippers get most of their property from auctions. They bid for properties with other investors hoping to win the bid at a low price within their budget. These homes may be falling apart, have countless costly problems, and is in an existing non livable condition. There could be core problems such as electrical, structural, and plumbing. Besides that investors have to fix the layout of the homes and bring it to a more salable condition. Homes may have an outdated layout for that location, and may need to be redesigned. Investors should seek professional assistance when needed. An architecture, contractors, professional designers are just some of the necessary work partners. An investor's vision of their new layout may not be feasible. The only way they would know this is by using a professional to assist in making that vision comes true. Investors need to know if they could remove or add a wall, or to legally make an addition, or stage the home in such a way to draw in buyers. It is not wise to assume that investors can do all these things themselves, even if they have the knowledge to do so. A second opinion is always the best way to go.

There are probably more investors engaging in rental properties than flipping them. Both are risky activities. Rental properties can be of a different scale. Some people buy a home to live in one part and rent out another to help with the mortgage payments. Because they live in one, they normally do the maintenance work themselves. If you do not want to maintain the property yourself, then a larger investment property should be your aim. A four family or more, may demand more maintenance work in which you need to employ a third party company specializing in maintaining investment properties. Some people may even hire a caretaker to live on site and take care of the dwelling. They will report to the investor of the existing conditions and the repairs that are needed. It should be completely understood that investment money and personal money should be completely separated. Larger apartment complexes have a whole team of management to run the complex. The more you spend, the bigger the dwelling, the more you should expect your responsibilities. Laws are also something you must take into consideration, when investing in rental properties. You have to address fair housing issues, insurance liability issues, and employment issues. Making money is hard work, but is well worth the work if you do it properly. The reason why people get involved in investment properties is for the money. It is the desire to live comfortably or extremely well, that drives investors. The fact is investors enjoy living rich. Who wouldn't?

Chapter 19

Your Next Move

<u>Will</u>

Loving your home, caring for your home, understanding your investment, and sharing it with others must make you wonder what happens if it is lost or if something happens to you where you can no longer keep it. What happens when you take ill or even worse? What happens if you die? Do you just forget about it and leave it? What do you do?

You should prepare for the worst and expect the best. It is the general rule of thumb. Having great expectations and dreams in your life is natural. Dream big and execute those dreams, providing you don't hurt others. With life, anything can happen. Life is about dreaming, about living, and about feeling. At some point things do stop or something interrupts the flow of it all. Not everyone is fortunate to live a long, wonderful, fulfilling life. Each one of our paths is different. We sometimes try to prepare for the future. But some people like to live for today with no responsibilities in mind. They start thinking about future responsibilities when they begin a family and have children.

Lawyers will recommend that everyone, whether you have children or not, should have a will. All of the things you acquire in your life, you can't take with you. Most precious things can sit beside you when are buried, but it doesn't move with you. Moreover, it would be pretty difficult to place your home where you are buried. Throughout history people used to be buried on their very property. This is not the case now a days.

With careful planning, homes can be left to love ones. They can assume the responsibility of the home you invested in. Some people prefer that their children have it easier than how they lived. A home provides a certain security for children. Yet, things don't always go that way. An estate sale may occur and involve a mountain of issues. Even if you had a will and left your property to your children, they may disagree on how it would be handled. Some may want to keep the property in the family and others may want to sell it and recoup the monetary benefits. An estate sale may draw legal issues that prevent a smooth and quick sale. If the property has any historical value, it may increase the legal issues involving the sale. Who it belongs to, whether it should be sold, and how it should be handled may now be an exponential problem. Third parties may intervene and possibly take claim on historical properties. A will outlining as much detail to the property is highly encouraged. It would avoid most of these raised issues.

As a property owner, you must find the strength to prepare properly and address issues you may not want to foresee. Handle with care, should always be on your mind when you are dealing with your property.

PART SIX

The Story

Chapter 20

In Debra's Favor

Debra had just received her real estate license and wanted to dive into her work. She'd heard about how lucrative the business can be. She had high dreams and aspirations. Debra was a single mother who was working a full time job as an administrative assistant for a large corporation. She worked hard in trying to makes end meet, but with two children it was very difficult. Her financial situation was constraint, because she wasn't getting any child or spousal support from her ex-husband. Her ex-husband was receiving disability from the government. A friend of a friend had told her about becoming an agent. She made it appear as if it had a promising future. Sandy had told her that she knew others who were making at least $50,000 dollars from the industry.

"If you don't try it you won't know," Sandy said. "$50,000 dollars added on to my lousy $30,000 is a good bonus in my eyes."

"It sounds good, but is it really attainable?" Debra asked.

"Do you really think you are going to move up in this company? Even if you don't make that amount of money, you will make some extra money. I'm telling you, it's worth a try. We don't get overtime, but they want us to stay late and work for nothing." Sandy said.

"Well, that's the union. It's part of our contract with them. Only certain positions make overtime. We're considered management." Debra explained.

"How are we management? We don't make six figures. We don't make anything. Its bull shit and the union is bull shit. I'm fed up. We just have to do things for ourselves or we will never get ahead. We're the ones suffering here, you know?" Sandy said.

"I know what you mean. I'm sick of it too, but I have to be

grateful that I have a job." Debra said sarcastically. "We're always reminded of that. Every time we have these meetings, they talk about how the corporation is just not going to hold up. They are always saying that they have to cut jobs and make changes. I'm tired of it. It's nerve racking." Debra said.

"So be financially independent. So try this real estate thing. It's like having your own business without having to come up with big money. Try it." Sandy continued to persuade Debra. It was working. Debra felt she had no choice, but to try another means of securing her future.

It was difficult to take the real estate classes, because child care was extremely expensive and difficult to come by. She had to find child care for the usual after school hours, but then there were the additional hours she needed for the classes she took at night. She hoped that it is worthwhile in the end.

There was an ad in the Penny Pushers, a local small advertising listings newspaper, for a real estate company looking for newly licensed agents. She decided to make an appointment with White House Realty.

Debra went right after work to her appointment with Julius of White House Realty. She was a bit nervous and was totally unprepared. She didn't bring her cover letter that she worked on the night before. Her children had distracted her. Fortunately she had her resume, but it didn't have her last revisions. It was a hot day, and she worked her ass off as usual from her day job. Her hair was a bit dis-shuffled and her make-up was a bit sweaty. She just didn't have any time to fix herself because she was running late.

"Hi, I'm Debra. I have an appointment with Julius." Debra greeted the receptionist with a smile. They met in a separate room away from the busy office activities. She saw that there were lots of agents running about and doing their thing. They were making phone calls, printing documents, and debating with one another. She thought that soon that would be her, engaged in the same activities. Julius was well dressed, well mannered, and extremely professional. He presented himself as a gentleman by offering to seat her.

"Busy day?" He asked. He saw that she was a bit exhausted and disoriented.

"Yes," she said.

"I won't take up too much of your time. I would like to explain to you a little bit about our agency and then what we expect from all our agents..." he began to go over the history of his agency and what their projected goals are. He wanted to assure that she understood that they were only interested in gaining agents that were on the same path. He took a look at her resume, but places no emphasis on it. Then he smiled. "So, tell me a little about yourself and what you are looking for from us."

Debra's heartbeat was racing at this point, for she was not expecting a question like that. She has not been on an interview for over 10 years. She forgot what she is supposed to do and how she was supposed to be prepared.

"Well, as you see on my resume, I have a full time job as an administrative assistant. My interest grew in real estate because I have a passion for the industry. My ex-husband had introduced me to the industry because he was involved in investment properties. Well I figured I should learn the industry as well, since I helped him out during our marriage..." Debra continued to elaborate on how she was so fascinated in the industry and made many implications that she had prior hands on experience, which she really did not. She needed the job and she would say anything to get the job. Julius telephoned her the next day and welcomed her to White House. She went to her second meeting where he outlined that she had to attend regular office meetings, cover the front desk from time to time, and is required to do open houses for office listings. She agreed to all of these.

A month had gone by where Debra had no listings and no buyers. She had attended all of the weekly office meetings, where other agents volunteered her to take the minutes. She had to cover the front desk two Saturdays, because the receptionist had gone on her vacation and they badly needed someone to handle the phones without creating chaos. Julius knew that she had administrative experience and thought she was the perfect candidate. No extra money was given to her. Moreover, she was fortunate enough to attend an open house with an office listing agent. Unfortunately, she wasn't able to share any of the prospects from the sign in sheet. A month went by and she thought she was getting nowhere. She met with Julius to discuss her monthly one on one progress for new agents.

"Let me begin to say, that you are doing very well here. We see that you have made exceptional efforts to fit in to our agency. We see a future for you here, but let's talk about your goals and how you wish to achieve them." Julius said. She was glad that now she showed her loyalty and Julius was going to help her make money. Julius took out a worksheet for her to fill out. "I would like you to fill in this sheet; showing me how much you want to make and what kind of sales you want to focus on. Also, think about the territory you would like to work."

"OK. And then?" Debra asked.

"Then we can discuss how you are going to do it. Call me and we can go further. You know that you may have to invest in some marketing materials, right? You already have a business card and a place on our office website. Yet, you need to make more effort in marketing yourself. Your success depends on your hard work." Julius stressed.

The next month she was able to get a buyer, Nancy, to work with. She was very happy. Her client was an elderly lady looking to down size. Her home had gotten too big and lonely. All of her family has moved out and her husband had recently passed. She wanted a smaller property that she can handle, preferably a condo. She signed an exclusive right to represent with Debra, not clearly understand what it really means. They went to view a lot of condo's, coops, and house rentals. Still Nancy wasn't satisfied with any. She was getting frustrated in running around with Debra. Debra, she thought, didn't understand her needs. So far she saw properties that had more than one bedroom which she did not want, rentals which she wasn't looking for, and coop's which she wasn't interested in entertaining. Debra, too, was getting frustrated with Nancy. She just couldn't find her exact wish list, so she thought anything close to it would do. But Nancy was very stubborn and wouldn't bend to other options.

"Look. I don't think this is working out. We just can't find anything." Nancy said. She was through with Debra.

"I'm sure I can find you something. You still have a month to work with me according to our representation agreement. I know I can find you something. We just need to go over your list again and see if we can fine tune it." Debra said.

"I just don't have the energy to go on so many viewings with no luck. Can't you just send me the information, so I can see it before you make the appointment?" Nancy asked.

"Of course, but you don't have an email. You said you don't use computers. How would I send it to you?" Debra asked. She thought this lady was very difficult and impossible. How can she ask to get information when she has no modern means in obtaining it? "I think we should go over your list and identify the things you must absolutely have. There is so much property out there that falls under your general criteria, so we need to weed through them. Please, let's try to do this another way." Debra pleaded.

Nancy was exhausted. She wanted to give up looking, but she just couldn't keep up with her expenses alone. It was becoming very pressing to find a more manageable home.

"OK, we can go over my list again." Nancy said. They went over the list and ruled out a lot. Most of her list consisted of all her current amenities, which just wasn't going to be there in a smaller home. It was truly unrealistic for the price range she wanted.

Debra was able to find three condos that Nancy agreed to. Nancy had to choose the one that best fits her, but wanted some advice from Debra. The first condo was in a gated community, with amenities for all ages, but had no available parking for her car. The second condo was further from the location she wanted and was hard to get to if her family wanted to visit. She had parking and very limited, poor quality, amenities. The third condo was a little over her budget, in walking distance to the market area, with no parking, and no amenities. Debra preferred that Nancy take the third condo, because it would yield her the greatest commission. Yet, she didn't stress her decision too much, because she made sure she took care in finding condo's in elderly Hispanic communities, which Nancy would fit right in.

"I think you should go with the condo in walking distance to the market. It's not really me to say, but if I was you that is the one I would go with. To me that neighborhood is extremely safe, great school district, and not far from the hospital. It has everything you will need at your fingertips. Believe me I looked very hard for you and to me that is the best choice." Debra said. Nancy couldn't help feeling that she was getting older and that maybe Debra is right. What if some emergency happened? What if she needed assistance from others? Everything was in her grasp and the community understood her language. She wouldn't have to strain to speak English; she could speak her native tongue with ease. She would be among her own kind of people.

Debra put her offer in. The listing belonged to another agency, the Black House Realty. Unfortunately, the Black House Realty and the White House Realty have always been rivals. Both are very competitive and have increased their shares in the market. They both had alliances with other realties. Debra got back a counteroffer with a firm sales price. She knew that Nancy couldn't afford the full asking price, and the other two listings of her choice now had accepted offers. She had no choice but to negotiate with the listing agent. This was the first time she had to deal with counteroffers and negotiations. She didn't want to go to Julius for help, because she had heard that they would give her less commission; if she had to seek help from any other agent. She called Lisa, the listing agent.

"Hi, Lisa." Debra began. She explained that her client is very much interested in the property and wanted the real deal on the seller's ambition to sell.

"What do you mean 'real deal', Debra?" Lisa asked.

"I mean what is the lowest your seller will accept? Be honest." Debra said.

"To be honest, I don't know who you think you're talking to. I have a responsibility to my client to represent her with her interest in mind. She is firm with her asking price and she is considering increasing it, because she has received a lot of competitive offers." Lisa said. "Most importantly I have to present all offers to her, so please send in your best and final offer."

Debra was nervous after speaking to Lisa. She didn't think that Nancy could truly afford that property. She didn't know what to do. She would have to start all over in the search, which she did not want to do. She decided to ask Nancy if she could put in a higher offer. Maybe if Nancy went to a different mortgage broker, she would qualify for the condo. She had made connections with a mortgage broker who had visited the office and thought that she would speak to him to see if he could give Nancy a pre-approval to meet the asking price.

"David, I really need you to do me a favor. I'm kind of in a bind. My client really wants this property, but I'm afraid the mortgage broker she was working with is really stingy with her. I thought that maybe you can give her a better deal. I can send you over the listing information. What do you think?" Debra asked.

"I think anything is possible. Why don't you email me the listing information and have her contact me so that I can proceed with the process. I can get you a pre-approval as soon as possible." David said.

"Thank you. You are a life saver." Debra was relieved. Now she had to speak to Nancy and convince her to contact David so that she can get a better pre-approval.

Nancy was nervous to hear that she was counter-offered with the asking price and that they were considering increasing the price. Debra also told her that the other two choices already had accepted offers that were in contract. It appeared that she had no choice and that she would have to start her search over. "Just forget the whole thing. I'm done working with you. You told me that that particular condo was the one to go with. You told me that even if it was overpriced, we can put an offer that was favorable to me. You told me that it was sitting on the market for some time and it would be an easy deal. Now you're telling me that they are increasing the price? Now you are telling me that they refused my offer? Now you are telling me that I don't even have an alternative. You've been making mistakes all through this. I'm going to have to speak to your broker about you. You're the worst agent there is and I am surely going elsewhere." Nancy said. She was infuriated.

"Nancy, please, calm down. I have a solution. Your mortgage guy, I think, doesn't know what he is doing. I'm not a mortgage lender, but I have spoken to one who says that based on your situation you can qualify for a lot more. Of course, it's up to you to work with him. He has worked with other clients of mine and was successful with them. Believe me I was able to find, very easily, the property of their dreams. It's very difficult to deal with your budget, where it is now. Can you just trust me? The worst that can happen is that you still have that other pre-approval." Debra said.

Nancy was tired. She had come this far and thought it was worth a try. If unsuccessful, she will report Debra. "OK, fine. What's the guy's name?" Nancy rudely asked. Debra gave her David's information and hoped for success. David was able to pull it off. He was able to approve Nancy for much higher than her initial approval. Nancy was extremely happy and thought Debra was a wonderful agent. Maybe she was being too hard on Debra, after all finding a home was no easy task.

Debra quickly put in Nancy's offer for the asking price, knowing she now has room to increase her offer if she had to. She was extremely confident that she would have a successful transaction and finally her first sale. The Black House Realty counter-offered again with the new asking price.

"Lisa, I wasn't aware that the listing price has increased. I know that you said it might change, but I didn't see any change on the MLS. Don't you have to make that change visible to all agents?" Debra asked.

"I did put it through. I don't know why the Board of Realtors is taking a long time. Maybe something is wrong with their system. But I have proof that I faxed in the information." Lisa said.

"OK. I'll let my buyer know of the changes. Where is our position in this, if we go with a higher offer? Has anyone else put in additional offers?" Debra asked.

"I'm still getting offers in, I can't say at this moment. Put in another offer if your client is still interested." Lisa said. After some careful explaining that the listing agent was playing hard ball, Debra convinced Nancy to put in a higher offer to secure the transaction. The next day, Lisa called Debra.

"Is this your best and final offer?" Lisa asked.

Debra didn't know for sure what to say, she replied "Is your client counter-offering again?"

"I just need to know if this is your best and final offer." Lisa asked.

"How can you ask me that question? You didn't tell me to put in the best and final offer. You only told me that you are counter-offering. You're not being fair Lisa." Debra complained.

"I told you that you should put in your best and final offer. It was very clear. I am going to take this as your best and final offer, since you can't give me an answer. My client wants to make a decision today." Lisa said.

"Wait. I forgot to mention to my client to put in her best and final offer. Can I get back to you in a minute?" Debra asked. Frustrated with how things are going. Debra attempted to contact Nancy, but she did not respond in time. She took it upon herself to put in an offer before it was too late. She already knew what Nancy could afford. Lisa called her back to tell her that her client accepted her best and final offer and they could proceed with the contract. Debra was relieved, but still has not heard from Nancy.

Later Debra found out that Nancy had taken ill and was admitted into the hospital. Her daughter called Debra to tell her that her mother will be out of the hospital in two days. Debra told her of the circumstances and that Nancy had successfully secured a condo. Nancy went to see Debra. She was with her daughter and walking with a cane.

"I'm so sorry for what happened. I didn't mean for you to come in. I could very well come to you. Are you feeling better?" Debra said.

"Oh don't worry about me. It comes with age. So I got the condo?" Nancy asked.

"Yes, you did. Are you excited?" Debra said with

enthusiasm.

"I am. I can't tell you how much this means to me. I can't wait until this is finished. It's been a while now." Nancy said.

"Yes. Well here is the paperwork. I'll go over it with you." Debra explained all the paperwork that Nancy had to sign. She went quickly over the price that had changed since the last time Nancy saw it.

"Wait a minute. I thought we put in an offer less than that? What happened? I didn't agree to this?" Nancy said.

"What do you mean? You agreed to this price. That's the price you told me to put in. Don't you remember?" Debra said.

"What? I don't remember any of this. I didn't tell you this. This price is too high." Nancy complained.

"Maybe you don't remember since your hospitalization, but we spoke over the phone about the counteroffer and you told me to go ahead and put in a verbal. I did exactly what you wanted. I just need you to sign the papers. I did everything ask of me." Debra said.

"I'm not stupid. And I didn't lose my mind Debra. I simply had a fall. That's all. What do you think, I hit my head? I didn't agree to this and I didn't get any calls about this new price." Nancy said.

"Mother, she did leave a message for you to call her. It was a couple of messages. Are you sure you didn't speak to her?" Nancy's daughter wasn't certain about her mother's memory.

"I know what I'm talking about. I'm not going to sign this. I don't like how you do business. From the start you have been behaving inappropriately. I'm not buying that property. If I have to go through this again, I just won't buy anything. I'll just stay in my home. I'm fed up with all of this." Nancy said sternly. She left with her cane and her daughter. Debra couldn't believe it. Now she didn't know what to do.

Lisa called her to find out about the paperwork.

"You would not believe it Lisa." Debra said nervously.

"What?" Lisa asked.

"My client couldn't be reached. And I just found out that she passed away. She was an elderly lady and sickly." Debra said.

"Oh my goodness. I'm sorry to hear that. I guess we just don't have a deal. I'll let my client know to consider the other offers." Lisa said.

Debra was relieved that she was off the hook and her broker didn't find out anything.

Lisa searched the obituaries in the newspaper for Nancy's information, but couldn't find anything. Lisa later sent out just listed marketing materials in Nancy's neighborhood. Nancy saw the condo she had wanted for the price she could initially afford. She immediately called Lisa to find out if she can put in an offer. Lisa went out to see her and had her sign the necessary documents of representation. She then told her that she was also representing the seller, so she was in a dual agency relationship. Nevertheless, she reassured Nancy that her client is eager to sell. Lisa made the transaction seamlessly and thanked David for the quick pre-approval that Nancy needed.

Nancy was very happy in her new condo.